THE RIVER THAMES
from Hampton Court *to the*
Millennium Dome

LAMBETH · BRIDGE

GW00705951

CADOGAN

Cadogan Guides
West End House
11 Hills Place
London W1R 1AH
guides@cadogan.demon.co.uk

The Globe Pequot Press
6 Business Park Road, PO Box 833, Old Saybrook,
Connecticut 06475-0833

Conceived and produced for Cadogan Guides by
The Jacket Front Ltd
postmaster@bookprodservices.demon.co.uk
Designed by Ann Burnham
Cover design by Fielding Rowinski

Written by Vanessa Letts

ISBN 1-86011-701-5

A catalogue record for this book is available from the British Library

Colour reproduction by
The Setting Studio, Newcastle upon Tyne
Printed in China by
Leo Paper Products Ltd

Photo Credits
The publishers would like to thank Vanessa Letts, who
supplied her own photographs, and also the following:
Hampton Court Palace: © Crown Copyright, HRP. Strawberry Hill, Orleans House:
Richmond upon Thames Tourism. Marble Hill House: © English Heritage.
Richmond Bridge, Richmond Park, Syon House: Richmond upon Thames Tourism.
Royal Botanic Gardens Kew: © Royal Botanic Gardens Kew. Kew Bridge Steam
Museum. Harrods Depository: Tricia Topping Associates Limited. Chelsea Physic
Garden. Chelsea Bridge Bungee Jump: UK Bungee Club. The London Baloon
Ride. Tate Gallery: Marcus Leith. Museum of Garden History: © Jerry Harpur. The
Houses of Parliament: © Parliamentary Copyright 1995, House of Commons
Education Unit. British Airways Millenium Wheel: Paul's Cathedral: © Unichrome
of Bath, © Judges Postcards Ltd, and John Buckler.. The Globe Theatre: Richard
Kalina. The Golden Hinde: © Golden Hinde Ltd. Monument: The Tower Bridge
Experience. The Old Operating Theatre: Great Museum Southwark. London
Dungeon. Winston Churchill's Britain at War Experience. Tower of London: ©
Crown Copyright, HRP. Bramah Tea and Coffee Museum. Design Museum: ©
Jefferson Smith. Royal Naval College: Greenwich Borough Council.

Contents

Hampton Court

The palace's riverside façade is exactly as it was in Tudor times.

HAMPTON COURT

Open Mar-Oct, Tues-Sun 9.30-6, Mon 10.15-6; mid Oct-mid Mar, Tues-Sun 9.30-4.30, Mon 10.15-4.30; adm £8.50, concs £6.40.

Like many a bouquet of flowers, Hampton Court was a peace offering. Cardinal Wolsey, the wily strategist whose arrogance and ostentation won him too many political enemies, tactfully gave the palace to Henry VIII in 1526. Henry graciously accepted the gift and then, when Wolsey failed to secure him a divorce from Catherine of Aragon, had him arrested for high treason.

Five of Henry's wives were brought to live in the palace, including Anne Boleyn, Jane Seymour and Catherine Howard. But Henry's most enduring love was Hampton Court itself and he added a Great Hall, a real tennis court (where the game is still played), vast kitchens and a grand astronomical clock.

When William and Mary came to live in Hampton Court in 1688 they recruited Christopher Wren to transform it into a second Versailles. Luckily only part of Wren's intended scheme was completed, and the palace's riverside façade is exactly as it was in Tudor times. William decorated the new apartments with paintings by Verrio, Gobelin tapestries and Delftware, restored the phenomenal Mantegna *Triumphs of Caesar*, and redesigned the gardens, adding a herb garden and the famous maze.

Twickenham & Richmond

KINGSTON BRIDGE

Jerome K. Jerome kept his boat at Kingston, and Kingston Bridge was the starting point for the river journey to Oxford described in his novel *Three Men in a Boat*. A stone bridge was built across this point as early as 1170; Kingston itself is one of the four oldest royal boroughs, and a prehistoric stone outside the Guildhall is thought to be the Coronation stone on which seven Anglo-Saxon kings were crowned.

Walpole bought the small coachman's cottage in 1747 and renamed it Strawberry Hill.

STRAWBERRY HILL
Open Apr-Oct for guided tours Sun 2-3.30, also by appt, tel 0181 892 0051, adm £3.50.

This batty building was the eccentric creation of Horace Walpole, the father of the English 'Gothick' novel. Walpole bought the small coachman's cottage in 1747, renamed it Strawberry Hill and spent the next fifty years turning it into a castle. Tombs, cloisters and ruined abbeys from England and Italy were lovingly copied and remodelled into doorways, ceilings, quatrefoil windows, fireplaces and chimney-pieces. By the 1760s it had become a chic tourist attraction; and Walpole printed his own entrance tickets and received visitors dressed in a lavender suit and silver waistcoat.

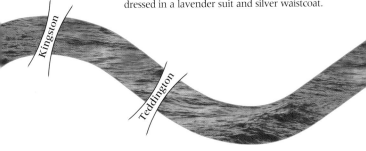

Kingston

Teddington

Twickenham & Richmond

ORLEANS HOUSE GALLERY

Open Tues-Sat 1-5.30, Sun 2-5.30,
closes 4.30 Oct-Mar, free.

The name commemorates the Duke of Orléans, later restored as King Louis Philippe, who fled the mass executions of the French Revolution to live in exile here from 1800–17. In 1927, nearly all the building was demolished, but James Gibbs' elegant Octagon Room was saved at the last minute and is now an art gallery.

MARBLE HILL HOUSE

Open Apr-Sept 10-6 daily; Oct-Mar 10-4
Wed-Sun; adm £3, concs £2.30.

This restrained Palladian villa was built in secret for Henrietta Howard, the 'respectable' mistress of George II. For Henrietta the house was a bolt-hole from the pressures of life at Court, where she had to juggle the demands of George II (for whom she was more trophy than lover), his wife and her own intemperate husband. Back at Marble Hill Henrietta attracted a more congenial set of friends including Horace Walpole, Jonathan Swift, John Gay and her next-door neighbour Alexander Pope. These days summer concerts are held in Marble Hill's riverside park.

The house was a bolt-hole from the pressures of life at Court.

Richmond

Twickenham & Richmond

RICHMOND LOCK & BRIDGE

When old London Bridge was demolished in 1832, the usual tidal flows altered and this stretch of the Thames shrank to little more than a trickle. After protests from residents a retractable dam was built to keep water levels high at low tide.

Richmond Bridge, a short way upriver from the lock, dates from 1777. It is London's oldest surviving bridge and the one that inspired Wordsworth's lines: 'Glide gently, thus for ever glide / O Thames! that other bards may see / As lovely visions by thy side / As now, fair river! come to me.'

London's oldest surviving bridge, the one that inspired Wordsworth.

RICHMOND DEER PARK

At 2,500 acres, Richmond is London's largest and wildest park. Richmond had been a popular hunting resort for sovereigns since medieval times but in 1637—shortly after moving to Richmond to avoid an outbreak of the plague—Charles I enclosed the land with an 8-mile-long brick wall. The deer chase he created was reserved for the sole use of the king and his court until 1751 when the wall was smashed down and the park given back to the public. These days its unspoiled tracts of grass, wetland, bracken and ancient oak-woods are home to about 700 fallow and red deer. They are free to roam throughout the park and, sadly, do so well there has to be an annual cull.

Twickenham

Kew

The Great Conservatory …was the inspiration for Joseph Paxton's Crystal Palace.

SYON HOUSE & PARK

House open April-Oct, Wed-Sun 11-5;
gardens open daily 10-dusk;
adm to both £5.50, concs £4.00..

Like many stately homes, Syon House has been turned into a small but cheerful theme park. It contains a trout fishery, aquarium, indoor adventure playground, miniature steam railway, garden nursery and the London Butterfly House. The house was originally a convent, but was purloined by Henry VIII and used to imprison his fifth wife, Catherine Howard, shortly before her execution. A friar had predicted that dogs would lick the king's blood in revenge for his treatment of the nuns, and when Henry died the prophecy came true. The funeral cortège stopped at Syon: during the night the coffin burst open and the next morning the household found dogs gobbling up the king's remains.

The house was given to the Percys in 1600, and has remained in the family ever since. In the 1760s it was resurrected by Robert Adam, who remodelled all the interiors, and Capability Brown, who landscaped all the grounds. One of Syon's finest buildings, however, is the Great Conservatory, designed in the 1820s by Charles Fowler, which was the inspiration for Joseph Paxton's Crystal Palace.

Kew

KEW GARDENS

Open 9.30-dusk, adm £5, concs £3.50,
children £2.50.

With 38,000 species of plants and trees set amongst palm houses, follies, an orangery and a 17th-century palace, these are the most exotic gardens in the world. Princess Augusta, the mother of 'Mad' King George, first planted the botanical collection in the

...extravagant follies, temples and summer-houses, the most famous of which is the 163ft-high Chinese Pagoda.

grounds of Kew Palace (a red-bricked Tudor mansion built on the river in 1631, closed for renovation until 2001). George III was as keen on the gardens as his mother, and it was he who first opened them to the public and commissioned William Chambers to build its extravagant follies, temples and summerhouses, the most famous of which is the 163ft-high Chinese Pagoda. In 1840 the gardens were given to the state and greatly expanded: Decimus Burton's spectacular glasshouses were built and plant laboratories set up which are still in use today. In one of the ten climate zones of the recently built Princess of Wales Conservatory is the Titan Arum, which at two metres high is one of the biggest flowers in the world. The Arum flowers once every 2–4 years and blossomed for the first time in 1996, exuding a horrible stink which clung to the clothes of newspaper photographers.

Kew

Kew

KEW BRIDGE STEAM MUSEUM
Open daily 11-5, adm £3.80,
concs £2.50, children £2,
all prices £1 cheaper on weekdays.

In the 19th century, this 197ft standpipe tower pumped 22.6 million gallons of Thames water a day to homes in west London. The lively museum inside the station owns five giant Cornish beam engines, two of which are started up on weekends at 3pm. The engines can be walked through while in steam, as can a section of Thames Water Ring Main in the excellent Water for Life Gallery documenting the history of water usage and supply in London. The highlight of any visit, however, has to be the 'Down Below' exhibition, a walk-through sewer which charts a complete history of sanitation from medieval times to the 20th century.

Kew Bridge, with its clean lines and sturdy structure, was built of Purbeck stone in 1903. On its left bank is the Strand-on-the-Green, a row of bijou cottages with steps leading up to the first floors as protection from flooding. Nancy Mitford, the arbiter of 'U' (upper-class) and 'non-U' behaviour, lived here in the 1930s.

CHISWICK BRIDGE

The elegant centre arch of Chiswick Bridge has the longest concrete span of any bridge across the Thames. On its southeast side is the Ship Inn and a towering 8-storey-high brewery where Budweiser beer is currently made—breweries have stood on the riverside manor owned by the Archbishops of Canterbury since 1427.

Kew

Chiswick

Hammersmith

Holst…lived in one of the 18th-century villas along the river.

BARNES BRIDGE

This attractive humpbacked railway bridge from 1849 was built out of pre-fabricated steel sections and includes a footway for pedestrians. Gustav Holst, composer of *The Planets* and a teacher at St Paul's Girls' School, lived in one of the 18th-century villas along the river from 1908 onwards. More recently, Marc Bolan, the lead singer of T-Rex, was killed in Barnes on 16 September 1977 after crashing into a tree on Barnes Common.

HAMMERSMITH BRIDGE

Designed by Joseph Bazalgette in 1887, Hammersmith Bridge is virtually a replica of the suspension bridge built here in 1827 by Tierney Clark (who famously built a bridge over the Danube connecting Buda and Pest). A memorial in the centre of the narrow bridge remembers the brave South African lieutenant who died in 1919 after diving into the river to save a drowning woman.

The artists Eric Gill, Eric Ravilious and William Morris all lived nearby, but these days Hammersmith is better known for its Riverside Studios (an innovative theatre and cinema complex on the river), and pretty riverside pubs (The Ship, The Dove, The Blue Anchor and The Black Lion) attracting swarms of sweaty merchant bankers in the summer.

Barnes

Hammersmith

Hammersmith

the same twin domes and salmon-pink terracotta façade as the Harrods store in Knightsbridge.

THE HARRODS DEPOSITORY

In the early 1890s Harrods bought an old soap factory in Barnes to use for furniture storage. The distribution warehouse pictured here was added in 1914 and has the same twin domes and salmon-pink terracotta façade as the Harrods store in Knightsbridge. In the late 1980s Harrods sold off the site and the depository has now been developed into 'Harrods Village', a compound of 250 townhouses and converted apartments selling from £235,000 for a 1-bedroom flat to £3 million for a riverside penthouse.

FULHAM FC

Fulham Football Club began as a church side (Fulham St Andrews) and moved to the grounds here at Craven Cottage in 1896. The club has never quite made it to the Premier Division, and the Cottagers' loyal fans still hallow the memory of 1905, Fulham's most successful season ever.

Hammersmith

Fulham & Putney

The prize possession is a preserved rat from the Plague of 1655.

FULHAM PALACE

Open Mar-Oct Wed-Sun 2-5;
Nov-Feb Thurs-Sun 1-4, adm 50p.

Tucked off Bishop's Avenue, in the grounds of Bishop's Park, this 13-acre plot has been owned by the Bishops of London since 704. The red-bricked Tudor/Georgian summer palace and 17th-century herb, botanical and kitchen gardens were opened to the public for the first time in 1973. Admission includes entrance to a quaint historical museum whose prize possession is a preserved rat from the Plague of 1665.

PUTNEY BRIDGE

Putney Bridge is the starting point for the annual Oxford & Cambridge Boat Race. The race between the rival universities spans a four and a quarter mile stretch from Putney to Mortlake and lasts 17 minutes, with each boat vying to dominate a narrow strip of water where the current flows fastest. Londoners crowd the bridges and pubs along the route and 500 million people watch the race live on TV.

Near the Star and Garter pub on the south side of the bridge is St Mary the Virgin, the Tudor church where the momentous Putney Debates were held in 1647. In these the Levellers (whose manifesto was to 'level all differences of position or rank among men') presented Cromwell with a radical new constitution. Though some of his own officers supported their proposals for universal suffrage and religious toleration, Cromwell rejected them and in 1649 he suppressed the movement completely. The transcript of the debates, written in shorthand, is the first public discussion of democratic rights on record.

Putney Bridge was built in 1886. Designed by Joseph Bazalgette and made of Cornish granite, it carried electric trams until 1930 when its width was doubled and the tram lines removed.

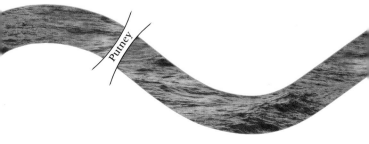

Putney

Chelsea & Battersea

WANDSWORTH BRIDGE

Wandsworth Bridge is the least glamorous but strongest of London's bridges. Opened in 1937, the steel-girdered bridge withstands a daily onslaught of heavy goods vehicles travelling in and out of London. On its south side is a popular pub called The Ship.

CHELSEA HARBOUR

This sleek riverside development includes a yachting harbour, 500 flats and houses (mostly occupied by film and TV people), a hotel, mall and offices. The whole lot was built in 1986 in less than 12 months. At its centre is Belvedere Tower, a 20-storey high pastiche pagoda with a flat to each floor and a computer-controlled golden ball at the top which falls and rises with the tides.

Wandsworth

Chelsea & Battersea

LOTS ROAD POWER STATION & CHELSEA REACH HOUSEBOATS

Coal is no longer delivered here by barge, but the massive belching chimneys of the Lots Road Station still generate enough electricity to power the entire London Underground. The houseboats moored next to Battersea Bridge in the foreground of this picture are a little town on the water, each one with its own postal address, electricity supply and cat.

ST MARY'S, BATTERSEA

London's only riverside church is often known as Blake's Church, because it was here in 1782 that the poet and visionary William Blake married Catherine Boucher, the daughter of a local market gardener. The present building dates from 1777 and replaced an even earlier church. A memorial inside commemorates Turner, who painted sunsets over the Thames from the vestry window.

Chelsea & Battersea

BATTERSEA BRIDGE

This gold and green iron bridge with its Victorian gas lights was built in 1890 by Sir Joseph Bazalgette, the engineer responsible for the Thames Embankments. It replaced a simple timber bridge of 1772, which Whistler depicted in his Nocturne in Blue and Silver (now in the Tate Gallery) shortly before it was demolished.

The row of mostly Queen Anne houses has become one of London's smartest addresses.

CHEYNE WALK

In the 19th century Cheyne Walk was home to George Eliot, Henry James, Elizabeth Gaskell, Hilaire Belloc, Marc and Isambard Brunel, Steer, Turner, Whistler, Swinburne, Meredith and Rossetti (who kept kangaroos, peacocks, owls and a wombat—supposedly the original of the dormouse in *Alice in Wonderland*—in his garden). The row of mostly Queen Anne houses has become one of London's smartest addresses, and the pastiche Tudor palace pictured here was built in 1998 at vast expense by a former deputy chairman of Lloyd's of London.

Battersea

Chelsea & Battersea

CHELSEA OLD CHURCH

The 'scholar, statesman, saint' Thomas More—executed in the Tower when he resisted Henry VIII's break with Rome—was a regular at Chelsea Old Church and built a chapel for his first wife in the grounds. In the Blitz of 1941, the church was blasted to 'nothing but an immense heap of timber and stone' and a German parachutist was found wandering on the nearby riverbank. The church has now been completely restored with the enigmatic addition of a lap-dancing statuette by Derwent Woodra in the adjoining gardens.

London's prettiest bridge …

ALBERT BRIDGE

London's prettiest bridge was designed by Rowland Ordish in 1873. The web of sugar-spun girders on which the bridge was hung was not strong enough to withstand this century's heavy goods vehicles and to avoid demolition the suspension bridge had to be shored up in the middle with two stone pillars. Albert Bridge still bounces under the traffic, and notices on the toll kiosks at either end advise soldiers to break step when marching over.

Albert

Chelsea & Battersea

CHELSEA PHYSIC GARDEN

Open Apr-Oct 12-5 Wed and 2-6 Sun, adm £3.50, concs £1.80.

The remarkable Physic Garden was founded in 1673 by the Society of Apothecaries for the 'manifestation of the glory, power and wisdom of God'. At the time most medicines were extracted from plants and even today the garden regularly supplies plant samples to pharmaceutical and fungal laboratories at Glaxo Wellcome and Imperial College. Chelsea Physic Gardens opened to the public for the first time in 1983, and crammed into an amazing three and a half acres you'll find the world's first rock garden, built from bits of Tower of London and Icelandic basalt lava, plus living woad (the blue dye used by the Romans), cotton seed (sent to Georgia from Chelsea to plant America's first cotton fields) and Britain's largest outdoors olive tree, which ripens in December and can produce a whopping 7lbs of olives in a single season. A statue in the garden commemorates Sir Hans Sloane, the physician, gardener and author of the famous Gardeners' Dictionary, whose heirs, the Cadogans, still own much of Chelsea.

The world's first rock garden, built from bits of the Tower of London.

BATTERSEA PARK & THE LONDON PEACE PAGODA

Open daily 8-dusk

Dickens described Battersea as 'a waste expanse' in 1842: it was a rough, marshy area, popular with vagrants and bums, and a notorious venue for fighting and duelling. Just over a decade later the marshes were filled in with a million cubic feet of earth (delivered by barge from the recently excavated Victoria docks) and laid out as a park. Now, with its joggers, roller-skaters and Dog's Home walkers, the park is one of the liveliest in London. There's an art gallery, a lake with cascades, a bandstand, deer enclosure and children's zoo. The park's most striking landmark is the golden Peace Pagoda, given to Battersea in 1985.

Albert

Chelsea & Battersea

The pensioners wear navy blue frock coats in the winter, scarlet in the summer.

CHELSEA ROYAL HOSPITAL
Open Mon-Sat 10-12 and 2-4 , Sun 2-4, free.

Four hundred old boys still live in the 17th-century home designed by Christopher Wren and founded by Charles II, supposedly after a one-legged veteran hobbled up to Nell Gwyn's coach begging for alms. The pensioners

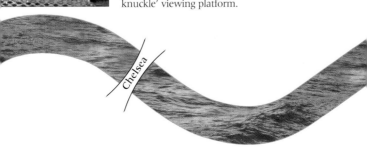

wear navy blue frock coats in the winter, scarlet in the summer, and three-cornered hats on special occasions (like Oak-apple Day in April, when the veterans adorn a statue of Charles II with oak leaves to commemorate the unsuccessful Battle of Worcester, in which the king hid in an oak tree to escape Cromwell and his troops).

THE CHELSEA BRIDGE BUNGEE JUMP
Open Fri 12-5 and Sat-Sun 11-6, closed
Fri Oct-Mar; adm £50 or £5 cage ride,
tel 0171 720 9496.

The ultimate in terror, this 300ft plunge leaves brave souls dangling above the Thames from the 'world's largest bungee tower'. For a mere £5, their less brave companions can watch them from a 'white knuckle' viewing platform.

Chelsea

Chelsea & Battersea

draped, Sloane Ranger-style, in a necklace of pearly lightbulbs.

CHELSEA BRIDGE

O pened in 1937, this suspension bridge was built out of prefabricated sections and is much stronger than Albert Bridge. Though plain and functional looking, Chelsea Bridge comes into its own at night when it is draped, Sloane Ranger-style, in a necklace of pearly lightbulbs.

CHELSEA TIDE-MILL

T he tide-mill works alongside this handsome water tower were installed by the Chelsea Waterworks Co., a private company formed in 1723. According to a petition to Parliament of 1827, the foul Thames water it extracted included 'the contents of the great common sewers, the drainings from dunghills, and laystalls, the refuse of hospitals, slaughter houses, colour, lead and soap work, drug mills and manufactories, and with all sorts of decomposed animal and vegetable substances, rendering the said water offensive and destructive to health …'. Londoners—who drink recycled river water to this day—can console themselves with the thought that efforts have been made to clean up the Thames in recent years and it is now inhabited by over 115 species of fish including chub, pike, anchovy, dory, haddock, mullet, sole, eel and salmon.

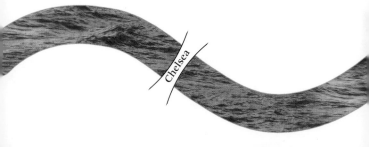

Chelsea

Vauxhall & Millbank

The power station has inspired a Pink Floyd album.

BATTERSEA POWER STATION

Dating from 1933, Battersea Power Station was the work of Sir Giles Gilbert Scott, the architect behind Bankside Power Station, Cambridge University Library and the classic British red telephone box. The solid-fuel power station has inspired a Pink Floyd album as well as countless Sunday painters, and is currently being turned into a multiplex cinema. Just behind it is Battersea Dogs' Home, a rescue home for stray dogs and cats founded in Islington in the 19th century.

VAUXHALL BRIDGE

The piers of Vauxhall Bridge, built in 1905, sport a set of Art Nouveau superheroes symbolising science, agriculture, architecture, engineering and pottery. On its south side is the Nine Elms fruit, vegetable and flower market which moved here from Covent Garden in 1974. Its warehouses, plus a new riverside housing development, stand on the site of Vauxhall Gardens, pleasure gardens which opened in 1660 inspiring emulators in Paris, New York, and St Petersburg.

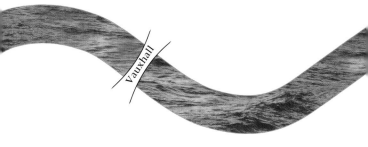

Vauxhall

Vauxhall & Millbank

Ballooning was a craze in 18th-century London.

THE LOCKING PIECE

The Locking Piece, a large, organic, fountain-washed bronze sculpture by Henry Moore, marks the point where prisoners from nearby Millbank Penitentiary were led down a flight of stone steps for deportation to Australia.

THE LONDON BALLOON RIDE

The helium-filled 'ballon captif' moored in Vauxhall Spring Gardens offers incredible panoramic views of the city from a maximum height of 400ft (rides cost £12 for 15 mins, open 10am–dusk, weather permitting; tel 0345 023842 for details). Ballooning—sometimes using hydrogen—was a craze in 18th-century London: 'Balloons occupy senators, philosophers, ladies, everybody,' wrote Horace Walpole in 1785.

Vauxhall

Vauxhall & Millbank

MI6

This self-consciously futuristic building, with its bottle-green walls, concrete spikes and cone-shaped trees, is the headquarters of MI6 and home to around 2,000 of Her Majesty's spies. A mesh or 'Faraday Cage' has been built into the fabric to prevent electromagnetic waves travelling in and out of the building, but MI6 has had to resort to more old-fashioned technology (blinds) to prevent sightseers in boats videoing the 007s downing gin and tonics in the riverside bar.

An unrivalled collection of 300 oil paintings and 19,000 sketches by Turner.

TATE GALLERY
Open Mon-Sat 10-5.50, Sun 2-5.50, free.

This outstanding collection of 20th-century art and British painting from 1500–1900 was founded originally by the great philanthropist Henry Tate, whose Tate & Lyle sugar-cube factory is the last of the riverside sites described in this book. When the modern collection moves to Bankside Power Station in 2000, the whole of the Tate will be devoted to British art, from definitive examples of Hogarth, Palmer, Constable, Blake and Stubbs, to the Tate's unrivalled collection of 300 oil paintings and 19,000 sketches by Turner. The Tate was built in 1897 on the site of Millbank Penitentiary.

Vauxhall & Millbank

MILLBANK TOWER

There was uproar in the press when the Millbank Tower—designed by Ronald Ward in 1960 and one of London's few attempts to copy the sleek glass curtain-walled skyscrapers of New York—was listed by English Heritage. The 387ft-high tower recently gained new notoriety as the nerve centre of New Labour when the party's apparatchiks, focus groups and media units moved here from dingy premises in the Walworth Road in 1997.

One of London's few attempts to copy the sleek glass curtain-walled skyscrapers of New York.

ALEMBIC HOUSE

Jeffrey Archer—London's aspiring Mayor and well-known author—lives in a penthouse at the top of this otherwise bland-looking building, surrounded by an eclectic £10m art collection which includes works by Lowry, Dufy, Sisley, Miro, Moore, Gerald Scarfe and Andy Warhol.

Lambeth

LAMBETH BRIDGE & PALACE

Horseferry Road on the north side of Lambeth Bridge commemorates the only place on the river where horses and coaches were allowed to cross by boat. The lucrative but

Horseferry Road commemorates the only place on the river where horses and coaches were allowed to cross by boat.

accident-prone monopoly was run by the Archbishops of Canterbury and only came to an end when Westminster Bridge went up in 1750. The present bridge, with its handsome pineapple obelisks and pylons, was built in 1932. At its south end is Lambeth Palace, home to the Archbishops of Canterbury since 1190 and partially rebuilt in the Gothic style in the 19th century. Also on the south bank of the river is the Thames fire brigade's Lambeth Floating Fire Station, towed here from Wales in 1991 and incorporating sleeping quarters, offices, a lecture theatre, kitchens and a gym.

ST MARY-AT-LAMBETH & THE MUSEUM OF GARDEN HISTORY
Open Mar-Dec, Mon-Fri 10.30-4, Sun 10.30-5, free.

This 14th-century church contains a unique museum of garden history centred around gardens planted in the 17th century by the collector and royal gardener John Tradescant, whose 'Ark' of weird and wonderful curiosities evolved into the Ashmolean Museum in Oxford. The cemetery contains the tomb of Captain Bligh, who was cast adrift with 18 men after the crew of the HMS Bounty mutinied.

Lambeth

ST THOMAS' HOSPITAL

Florence Nightingale, 'The Lady with the Lamp', was one of the innovative sparks behind the 800-year-old hospital's move to this site from Southwark in 1871. Although modern buildings have replaced much of the old, her famous training school for nurses remains; qualified 'Nightingales' wear the same caps, back to front, as their mentor.

THE HOUSES OF PARLIAMENT

The present building replaced the Royal Palace of Westminster, built originally by King Canute, then rebuilt and enlarged by Edward the Confessor and William the Conqueror. On 16 October 1834 a fire in the

Londoners cheered as the palace burnt almost completely to the ground.

furnaces beneath the House of Lords raged out of control and thousands of Londoners flocked to the scene in boats and cheered as the palace burnt almost completely to the ground. The following year Parliament decided to rebuild on the same site and a competition for a 'Gothic or Elizabethan style' replacement was won by the architect Charles Barry. He worked on the project for 25 years with the help of Augustus Pugin, the 24 year-old genius behind the entire building's dazzling Gothic ornamentation. Today a flag flying on top of the Victoria Tower, to the west, signifies Parliament is sitting.

Westminster

BIG BEN

Big Ben is supposedly named after Sir Benjamin Hall, the tall Commissioner of Works who was blamed for the catalogue of accidents and bungles which delayed completion of the tower until 1859. Big Ben has seldom stopped by accident, although the hands have been known to seize up with frozen snow and under the weight of flocks of starlings. The clock's pendulum is 13ft long: pennies regulate its swings to two-fifths of a second and a lamp in the lantern at the top indicates Parliament is sitting. The chimes are based on an aria from the Messiah, and the words accompanying the ding-dong-ding-dong are: 'All through this hour / Lord be my guide / And by Thy Power / No foot shall slide' (BONG).

WESTMINSTER BRIDGE & THE SOUTH BANK LION

For 700 years London Bridge was the city's only river crossing. Five lotteries were held to raise funds to build Westminster Bridge, which eventually opened in 1750. The toll-free bridge was the first of many to threaten the livings of an estimated 40,000 watermen who regularly plied for hire up and down the Thames. While Wordsworth dedicated a poem to it (Upon Westminster Bridge), James Boswell's consecration was more literal: '… I picked up a strong jolly young damsel,' the Scottish diarist wrote, 'and taking her under the arm I conducted her to Westminster Bridge, and then in armour complete [donning a condom] did I engage up in this noble edifice. The whim of doing it there with the Thames rolling below us amused me much.'

Keep an eye out for the 'South Bank Lion', who guards Westminster Bridge from a plinth on its southwest corner. The handsome beast was sculpted in Coade stone as a mascot for the old Lion Brewery (now the Festival Hall), and was moved to this spot after he survived the Blitz in perfect condition.

Westminster

THE EMBANKMENTS

On 30 June 1858 the House of Commons adjourned after a panic broke out over the 'great stink' of sewage coming off the Thames. To get rid of the smell, lime was piled into the river and river-facing windows of Parliament were hung with sheets soaked in lime chloride. A statue near Charing Cross Bridge commemorates Sir Joseph Bazalgette, London's Chief Commissioner of Works and the man who eventually tackled a situation which was precipitating cholera outbreaks in half the city's population. Bazalgette's brilliant solution was to bury London's open sewers underground and divert the sewage away from central London, from where most of the city's drinking water was still drawn, and out to the Thames estuary. The scheme, completed in 1875 at a cost of £6.5m, created the Victoria and Chelsea Embankments, an elegant, 3.5-mile stretch of riverside walkways and gardens decked out with cast-iron benches and black-painted dolphin lamps.

COUNTY HALL & THE LONDON AQUARIUM

Open Mon-Sun, 10-6, last adm 5pm
adm £8 adults, £7 concs, £6 children;
tel 0171 967 8000.

Home to the Greater London Council until Mrs Thatcher abolished it in 1986, this palatial building is now used to display a more colourful crowd of often bizarre creatures including giant groupers, piranhas, carpet sharks, stingrays, long-horned cowfish, jellyfish, sea horses and octopus. The fish live in a 3-storey high 2.5 million-litre basement aquarium complete with living coral reefs, mangrove swamps, rainforests, Easter Island 'ruins', trickling sound effects, and 'touch pools', where children can pick up and handle star fish, rays and mussels. The upper floors of this under-exploited building house a 200-room Marriott hotel, a McDonalds and a restaurant.

Westminster

South Bank & Charing Cross

The ferris wheel will be solar and wave-powered.

BRITISH AIRWAYS MILLENNIUM WHEEL
Opening 2000

Opening by invitation only on 31 December 1999, this is the British version of the sinister Giant Ferris Wheel in Vienna's famous Prater amusement park. The ferris wheel will be solar- and wave-powered and each 30-minute revolution will take up to 25 passengers on a 450ft arc into the city sky.

CLEOPATRA'S NEEDLE

This 3,500-year-old obelisk (a twin to the Cleopatra's Needle in Manhattan) was given to Britain by the Viceroy of Egypt in 1819. The 186-ton, 68ft-high monolith was carved by the Pharaohs in 1500 BC and stood in Alexandria during Cleopatra's lifetime. When it was put up on Embankment in 1878 a graffiti artist wrote: 'This monument one supposes / Was looked upon by Moses / It passed in time from Greeks to Turks / And was stuck up here by the Board of Works.' The Board buried two sealed time capsules under the obelisk containing a picture of Queen Victoria, several newspapers, four Bibles, some hairpins, Bradshaw's Railway Guide and photographs of England's twelve prettiest girls.

Hungerford

South Bank & Charing Cross

Two new footbridges will link the South Bank to the heart of the West End.

CHARING CROSS STATION & NEW HUNGERFORD BRIDGES

L ooking like a Viking's helmet, this imposing new office complex and railway shed was built on top of Charing Cross Station in 1990. The word 'Charing' probably comes from the Anglo-Saxon word *cerr*, meaning a bend in the river, and the 'cross' in Charing Cross refers to the last of the twelve crosses put up by Edward I to mark the route taken by the funeral cortège of Queen Eleanor of Castile. By spring 2000 two new Hungerford footbridges (pictured here) will link the South Bank to the heart of the West End.

THE FESTIVAL HALL & HAYWARD GALLERY

T he Royal Festival Hall with its distinctive lime-green roof is at the heart of the vibrant South Bank Centre. The concert hall was the only permanent building to come out of the Festival of Britain in 1951, but it was soon joined by the Hayward Gallery (used for international art exhibitions), the Queen Elizabeth Hall, the Purcell Room and the National Theatre. There are excellent free concerts in the Festival Hall foyer/airport lounge Wed–Sun, 12.30–2pm.

Hungerford

South Bank & Charing Cross

MUSEUM OF THE MOVING IMAGE
Open daily 10-6, adm £6.25, student £5.25, other concs £4.50; tel 0171 401 2636.

The entertaining Museum of the Moving Image is London's most interactive museum. Six amateur actors, dressed in period costume, can coax even the most bashful visitors into lying on a carpet with Superman, taking a Hollywood screen-test, making their own cartoon or reading the news. Permanent exhibits include Marilyn Monroe's shimmy dress from *Some Like it Hot*, Charlie Chaplin's hat and cane, a Freddie Mercury holomovie and a multitude of classic clips.

The biggest, newest and most technically advanced IMAX in Europe.

IMAX THEATRE
Open daily, entrance and adm via the Museum of the Moving Image.

Rising phoenix-like from a depressing roundabout outside Waterloo Station, this £20m glass drum is the biggest, newest and most technically-advanced IMAX in Europe. The 500-seat theatre inside will show a mix of 2D and 3D IMAX films on a 10-storey-high screen using a projector the size of two small cars. Films range from the stupendous concerts by the Rolling Stones, pounded out over an 18,000-watt sound system, and documentaries such as the critically-acclaimed *Everest*, to the wondrous and bizarre such as Paul Cox's *Four Million Houseguests*, a vertiginous journey via an illuminator super-microscope.

Waterloo

The bridge that inspired the Kinks' 'Waterloo Sunset' hit of 1967.

WATERLOO BRIDGE

With its lofty views of the Thames, St Paul's and the City, this is the bridge that inspired the Kinks' 'Waterloo Sunset' hit of 1967. The clean, utilitarian bridge was designed by Giles Gilbert Scott, the architect behind Battersea and Bankside Power Stations. It was finished just after war broke out in 1939 and replaced a handsome York stone Regency bridge of 1817 (it was privately owned and a toll of half a penny was charged to pedestrians). The timber pilings holding up the Regency bridge were in such good condition when they were hauled out of the riverbed clay that they

were recycled as decorative panels in trains owned by the London, Midland and Scottish Railway Co. Next to Waterloo Bridge, on the north side of the bridge, is the capital's only floating Thames Police Station. The Thames Police were set up in 1798 by the prison reformer Jeremy Bentham, but crime on the river is still rife and in 1997-8 divers and detectives from Thames Division recovered £3m-worth of boats and marine equipment.

Waterloo

South Bank & Charing Cross

An excellent collection of mainly Impressionist and post-Impressionist paintings.

SOMERSET HOUSE & THE COURTAULD GALLERY
Open Mon-Sat 10–6, adm £4, concs £3, students/children free, tel 0171 873 2549.

Somerset House dates from the 1770s and stands on the site of a grandiose Renaissance palace built in 1547 for the Duke of Somerset (Lord Protector to the 9-year-old King Edward VI). The handsome Georgian building has housed a range of public registers,

including births, marriages and deaths, since the 18th century. As well as the dreaded Inland Revenue, the building is now home to the Courtauld Institute's excellent collection of mainly Impressionist and post-Impressionist paintings (Van Gogh's Bandaged Ear, Manet's Bar at the Folies Bergère and Cézanne's Montagne Sainte-Victoire) alongside some exquisite examples of Cranach, Tiepolo, Bonnard, Modigliani and Taborn.

THE ROYAL NATIONAL THEATRE

If proof was ever needed that concrete does not suit the English climate, this is it. Fortunately the inside, incorporating three outstanding theatre spaces plus a labyrinth of foyers, cafés and bookshops, is much more welcoming.

South Bank & Charing Cross

LONDON TV CENTRE

The studios in this tower are used for recording such timeless productions as Blind Date, Barrymore, SMTV and Light Lunch (free tickets available on 0171 287 0045; but call at least a month in advance). With its cafés, restaurants and stalls selling sculpture, ceramics, fashion and jewellery, neighbouring Gabriel's Wharf is a good place to stop for drinks or snacks.

THE OXO TOWER

Oxo, the stock cube people, neatly side-stepped the strict advertising regulations of the 1930s by working the letters 'OXO' into the design of the tower itself. In 1996 the Art Deco warehouse was magnificently restored by the Coin Street Community Builders, and it now contains over 30 retail units selling high-

quality textiles, furniture, clothing and jewellery at a fraction of West End prices (try Studio Fusion for the finest enamelled jewellery in the country). Above the work-shops is a modestly priced café/bar (Bistrot 2) and several floors of co-op flats; at the very top is a public viewing gallery and the chi-chi Oxo Tower Restaurant and Brasserie.

Waterloo

The City & Bankside

The futuristic egg-shaped swimming pool will rise and fall with the tides.

THAMES LIDO

Opening 2001.

The steep flight of stairs just here was a kind of 18th-century taxi rank, used by ferrymen for setting down and picking up passengers crossing the Thames. The internationally famous Brazilian concert pianist Marcelo Bratke makes a hobby of beachcombing on the Thames, and can often be seen scouring this part of the river for an interesting variety of objects including gloves, bicycle tyres, brooms, bottles, glasses, prams and cones. In 2001 the new Thames Lido will be moored here at the end of a 130ft-long jetty. The futuristic egg-shaped swimming pool will rise and fall with the tides, giving swimmers 360° views of the city around them.

Blackfriars

The City & Bankside

Barristers inhabit the buildings of the Temple to this day, eating off a dining table made out of the hatch of the Golden Hinde.

THE TEMPLE & HMS WELLINGTON

The large stone archway here on the Embankment was designed by Sir Joseph Bazalgette to mark the Temple Stairs, a stone staircase leading down to the river where passengers could catch ferries to and from the City. Behind the stairs is the Temple, home from about 1160 to the Knights Templar, a military order dedicated to winning back the Holy Land from Muslim control who piqued themselves on fighting to the death. In the Crusades the knights turned their hands to moneylending, so successfully that the order was suppressed by the Pope in 1307 and then abolished. Lawyers and their students began to move into the Temple and in 1609 James I gave the property

to the Bar for use as chambers. Barristers inhabit the buildings of the Temple to this day, eating off a dining table made out of the hatch of the Golden Hinde, and blasting a horn at suppertime to call in members who were inclined to spend their afternoons fishing on the Thames. The flower beds of Temple Gardens are, according to tradition, where the Lords of York and Lancaster each plucked the red and white roses that became their emblems in the Wars of the Roses.

The City & Bankside

BLACKFRIARS BRIDGE

Blackfriars' fifteen minutes of infamy came on 15 June 1992, when the Italian banker Roberto Calvi was found hanging from its latticed girders with 11lbs of bricks in his pockets. Calvi's bank collapsed soon after and his

The name comes from an order of Dominican Black Friars established on the north side of the river.

financial adviser died of cyanide poisoning four years later. Whether Calvi was murdered or committed suicide is still not known.

Blackfriars is the widest bridge along the Thames, and one of the handsomest (though critics mocked its vulgar red granite pulpits when the bridge was put up in the 1860s). The name comes from an order of Dominican Black Friars established on the north side of the river in the 1220s (a company of Carmelite White Friars lived nearby). The area degenerated into one of London's rankest slums, partly because butchers and fishmongers working in Fleet Market dumped offal straight into the nearby River Fleet (which still flows into the Thames through a conduit next to Blackfriars Bridge). On the south side of the bridge is Doggett's Coat and Badge Pub, named after a boat-race for apprentice watermen held there in late July and dating back to 1715.

Blackfriars

The City & Bankside

LONDON, CHATHAM & DOVER RAILWAY CREST

The fat red columns in this photograph are piers from a railway bridge which was put up in the 1860s but dismantled twenty years later. The brightly painted London, Chatham & Dover Railway crest on the south side of the river came from one of the original abutments used to support the short-lived railway bridge.

MILLENNIUM BRIDGE
Opening spring 2000.

The elegant Millennium Bridge will be the first free-standing pedestrian footbridge to be built across the Thames for over a hundred years. Designed by architect Norman Foster, sculptor Anthony Caro and engineers Ove Arup, it will link St Paul's to Bankside's Tate Gallery of Modern Art.

Blackfriars

The City & Bankside

TATE GALLERY OF MODERN ART AT BANKSIDE POWER STATION

Opening May 2000, visitor's centre open now 10-5, by appt 0171 401 7302.

Looking like a set from Fritz Lang's *Metropolis*, this dour fortress was designed by Sir Giles Gilbert Scott in 1947. The power station is now being gutted and flooded with natural light via a glass canopy designed by the Swiss architects Herzog & de Meuron. The glass roof will span the entire building, adding two floors to its height and giving visitors spectacular views across the City. The 100,000 square feet of galleries inside will house three temporary loan exhibitions a year plus the whole of the Tate's modern art collection: Picasso (*The Three Dancers*), Matisse (*The Snail*), Bonnard, Brancusi, Dalí, Krasner, Pollock, Duchamp, Moore, Gabo, Giacometti, Warhol (*Marilyn Diptych*), Hockney, etc.

Millennium

The City & Bankside

ST PAUL'S CATHEDRAL

Open Mon-Sat 8.30–4, adm £4,
concs £2, tel 0171 236 4128.

St Paul's was one of 52 London churches rebuilt by Christopher Wren in the wake of the Great Fire of 1666. The church caught fire on 3 September 1666, generating such heat that the 250-year-old corpse of a Bishop of London, Robert Braybrooke, blasted out of its grave and landed in the churchyard. Four churches, the first dating from Anglo-Saxon times, had stood on the site and, from the laying of the first stone in 1675, the fifth incarnation took 35 years to complete. Ten years after it was finished the church commissioners added a balustrade to the outside of the dome. 'Ladies think nothing well without an edging' was Wren's only comment. His tomb, with the inscription 'Si monumentum requiris, circumspice' ('If you seek his monument, look around'), is in the south choir aisle. The venerable cathedral proved how sturdily it was made in the Second World War when 28 incendiary bombs bounced off the dome leaving it entirely unscathed.

Millennium

The City & Bankside

Short of throwing rotten eggs, audiences are encourged to join in as much as possible.

THE GLOBE THEATRE

Exhibition open daily, adm £5, concs £4
tel 0171 902 1500 for box office and further
information, café and grill restaurant.

Bankside was a honeypot of sin, from inns, hostelries and 'stews' or brothels, to the decadent playhouses and bull-baiting rings where tethered bulls were taunted by mastiff dogs. The barbarous killings were relished by citizens of every class, from the lowliest punters to Elizabeth I and her successors. The new Globe Theatre stands on the site of one Bankside's largest bull-baiting arenas, a few hundred feet away from the original Wooden O where *Romeo and Juliet, King Lear, Hamlet, Othello, Macbeth* and *The Taming of the Shrew* were all performed. With its pristine thatch and timber-frame and open roof, the new playhouse tries to stay as faithful to the spirit of Shakespeare as possible. Costumes are dyed in urine, some productions experiment with gender crossing and, short of throwing rotten eggs, audiences are encouraged to join in as much as possible. Four plays are staged in repertory every summer, and admission to the highly acclaimed performances is always cheap.

Southwark

The City & Bankside

On its south side is the Anchor Inn, patronised by Samuel Johnson in the 18th century.

SOUTHWARK BRIDGE

With its steel arches, granite piers and understated grace, Southwark Bridge opened in 1921 to replace an earlier toll-bridge. On its south side is the Anchor Inn, an enormous pub with five bars and two dining rooms, patronised by Samuel Johnson in the 18th century. The Anchor stands on the site of two brothels, The Castle on the Hoop and The Gonne, in what used to be London's most popular red light district. Nicknamed 'Winchester Geese', the whores were cruelly treated and worked in brothels owned and operated by the Bishops of Winchester. Next to Southwark Bridge, a railway bridge leads towards the two yellow bricked, Italianate spires of Cannon Street Station.

Southwark

The City & Bankside

THE GOLDEN HINDE

Open daily 9am-sunset, adm £2.30, concs
£1.90, children £1.50; tea and coffee available.

This Golden Hinde is a perfect replica of the galleon used by Sir Francis Drake to circumnavigate the world in 1580. Drake returned from his trip with £600,000 of South Seas booty (the equivalent of £60m today), having claimed 'Nova Albion' or California along the way. The original Golden Hinde rotted away in a berth in Deptford, and the Devon-built reconstruction you see here is actually a working galleon which has sailed many more miles across the world than its predecessor. A crew consisting of master, mate, cook and 12 deckhands lives aboard the ship.

THE MONUMENT

Open daily 10-6, adm £1.50, child 50p,
tel 0171 626 2717.

As you approach London Bridge, look out for the golden flames of the urn atop the Monument, a slim, free-standing column commemorating the Great Fire of London. Designed in 1677 by Robert Hooke (a friend of Christopher Wren's), it is 202ft tall and stands exactly 202ft east of the bakery in Pudding Lane where the fire broke out on 2 September 1666. 'Pish! A woman might piss it out!' the incompetent mayor of London spluttered when he was woken up in the night. But the fire blazed for three days, destroying four-fifths of the City of London and displacing 100,000 Londoners Pepys looked on in horror at ' poor people staying in their houses … till the very fire touched them, and then running into boats or clambering from one pair of stairs by the waterside to another.' Hooke's column was engraved with the words 'London Rises Again' and with an inscription blaming the fire on Roman Catholics which was quietly removed in 1830. Nowadays, visitors who manage to climb 311 steps to the top are awarded a fitness certificate.

London

The City & Bankside

LONDON BRIDGE

'London Bridge is falling down, falling down, falling down,' is an understatement. The bridge—London's only river crossing from Roman times until the 18th century—has fallen down at least eight times, most dramatically in 1014 when the Vikings tied ropes around the supporting posts and rowed with the tide until it collapsed. A stone bridge with 19 Gothic arches was built in 1176 and, like the Ponte Vecchio in Florence, it was crammed with shops and houses and even a chapel dedicated to St Thomas à Becket. Grisly looking

spikes at either end were used to exhibit the heads of executed traitors, including the Scots patriot William 'Mel Gibson' Wallace, the English rebel Jack Cade, and the saint and politician Thomas More (his head was dropped into a boat and carried away by his much-loved daughter, Margaret Roper). Holbein and Hogarth both lived on the bridge, but in the 1750s its shops and houses were demolished and in 1831 a new London Bridge took its place. When this too showed signs of giving way, it was dismantled and bought by an eccentric American, who transported it in 10,000 pieces to Havasu City, Arizona. A dull new bridge (pictured here) was built across the river in 1973.

London

The City & Bankside

THE OLD OPERATING THEATRE, MUSEUM & HERB GARRET

9a St Thomas' St, SE1, open daily,
10.30-5, adm £2.90, concs £2, child £1.50..

This mind-boggling time capsule was discovered by chance in 1957 when a historian squeezed through a tiny hole in the belfry of a chapel belonging to old St Thomas' Hospital. The operating room that Raymond

At this time amputations lasted 60 seconds or less and the patients had to be doped up on ale or opiates.

Russell found in the garret room above dates from 1822, before anaesthetics and antiseptic surgery were known. At the time amputations lasted 60 seconds or less and the patients had to be doped up on ale or opiates and held down by as many as half a dozen assistants. The incredible museum, with its original blood-stained floor and mop and bucket, includes a unique collection of surgical instruments and a medieval herb garret, used by the hospital's apothecary to store and prepare medicinal compounds.

THE LONDON DUNGEON

28 Tooley St, SE1, open 10-5.30 Apr-Sept,
10.30-4.30 Oct-Mar, adm £8.95,
concs £7.95, child £6.50.

This gorified haunted house contains an awesome range of high-decibel low-octane schlock-horror rides including the 'Jack the Ripper Experience', 'Madame Guillotine' and 'Judgement Day'. Fortunately none of them are overly authentic.

Tower Bridge

OLD BILLINGSGATE FISH MARKET

Until Billingsgate Fish Market moved to the Isle of Dogs in 1982, fish had been sold from here since Saxon times. This market building, with its glittering goldfish weather vanes, dates from 1875 and was designed by Horace Jones. The market was bought by Citibank for use as a securities dealing room, but in 1987, just after it had been renovated by Richard Rogers, the stock market crashed and the building was abruptly abandoned.

HAY'S GALLERIA

In the 1980s these noble Victorian warehouses were joined together by a vaulted glass roof and converted into the ultimate retail-therapy haven, a tasteful shopping and eating piazza with a splashing fountain and a pleasant looking sculpture in the middle.

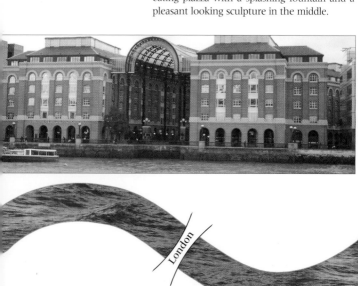

London

Tower Bridge

WINSTON CHURCHILL'S BRITAIN AT WAR EXPERIENCE

64 Tooley St, SE1, open daily Apr-Sept,10-5.30, Oct-Mar,10-4.30, adm £5.95, concs £2.95-3.95, tel 0171 403 317.

This nostalgic look-back at London in the Blitz includes a real Anderson shelter, a reconstructed Tube station and loads of memorabilia (authentic ration books, radio broadcasts, newspaper cuttings, etc).

HMS BELFAST

Open daily March-Oct,10-6, Nov-Feb, 10-5, adm £4.40, concs £2.20-3.30.

With its cold blue and grey camouflage and tall, menacing gun turrets, the Belfast is an austere but breathtakingly beautiful exemplar of military hardware. Built in 1938, the 11,500-ton battle cruiser saw active service from the outbreak of the Second World War (participating in the D-Day landings) until the end of the Korean War. Inside there are seven decks to explore, including boiler and engine rooms.

Plans are afoot to build a new City Hall for London in the shape of an enormous motorcyclist's helmet on the south bank of the river beside the Belfast. Designed by Norman Foster, the helmet will house the new Mayor of London and the Greater London Authority, a successor to the Greater London Council which was abolished in 1986.

The 11,500-ton battle cruiser saw active service from the outbreak of the Second World War until the end of the Korean War.

Tower

Tower Bridge

Up to 1,000 prisoners at a time were incarcerated within the Tower's walls.

TOWER OF LONDON
Open Mar-Oct, Mon-Sat 9-6 and Sun 10-6;
Nov-Feb, Tues-Sat 9-5 and Sun-Mon 10-5;
adm £9.50, concs £7.15, child £6.25.

The Tower was one of three castles raised on the Thames by William the Conqueror in 1066. Made of white Normandy stone with 15ft thick walls, the tall, imposing fortress was a mighty disincentive to aspiring English rebels.

In fact the Tower has never fallen and monarchs have merely added to it, building tower after tower along the inner and outer walls surrounding the original four-pronged stronghold. In its time the compound has housed a mint, arsenal, armoury, observatory, jewel house, lighthouse, records repository, bear-baiting arena, and state prison. Henry III contributed a menagerie including a French elephant, three German leopards and a Norwegian polar bear, kept on a chain so it could fish on the river. These were joined by lions, eagles, mountain cats and a jackal, until in 1834 one of the lions attacked a Beefeater and all the animals, except the ravens, were banished to London Zoo.

Most of the Tower's victims arrived via the river through Traitor's Gate, built for Edward I but subsequently used for receiving prisoners from Westminster. Up to 1,000 prisoners at a time were incarcerated within the Tower's walls, including Lady Jane Grey, Sir Thomas More, Bishop Fisher, Thomas Cromwell, Elizabeth I, the Earl of Essex, Sir Walter Raleigh and Guy Fawkes. Two of Henry VIII's wives, Anne Boleyn and Catherine Howard, were executed on Tower Green. The Tower's last prisoner was Rudolph Hess—Hitler's amanuensis and deputy Führer—who was held here for four days in 1941.

The Tower is also, of course, home to 38 Yeoman Warders (nicknamed Beefeaters because of their 2lb daily meat rations) and the Crown Jewels. Cromwell sold off nearly all the royal jewellery in the Civil War and, except for three swords and an anointing spoon, all the treasures on display here date from after 1660.

Tower Bridge

In its first year, the arms were lifted an average of sixteen times a day.

TOWER BRIDGE

Open daily, Apr-Oct, 10-5.15, Nov-Mar, 9.30-4.45, adm £5.95, concs and child £3.95.

This great galumphing bridge was built by two men, John Wolfe-Barry and Horace Jones. Jones designed the jolly mock-medieval stone exterior; Barry was the engineering genius behind the steel framework and the arms, or bascules, that rise up into the air to let tall ships pass below. The two arms, weighing 1,000 tonnes each, were originally lifted by steam engines housed in the base of the south-side tower. In its first year (1894–5) the arms were lifted an average of 16 times a day and even with the steady decline in river freight traffic in central London the bridge is still raised at least once a day (tel 0171 378 7000 to find out times). Admission includes entrance to the multimedia style Tower Bridge Experience, plus the original steam engine rooms and the high-level walkways built for pedestrian use when the arms were raised. These were closed for several years in 1910 after they became too popular with suicides.

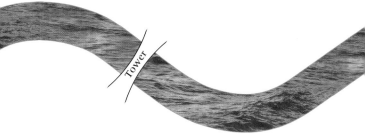

Tower

Docklands

ST KATHARINE'S DOCKS

There was an outcry when the development of St Katharine's Dock was announced in the 1820s. In the space of a month 1,250 houses including a 12th–century church and hospital were demolished and 11,000 people

St. KATHARINE DOCKS

made homeless. Tall yellow-bricked arcaded warehouses designed by Thomas Telford were built and used for storing wine, rum, dried fruit, dried flowers, tea, wool, ivory and indigo. Though only small, the basin could hold up to 1,000 ships and 1,0000 lighters (the flat-bottomed craft used for unloading ships). They stayed in use until 1968, and were the first to be redeveloped (with a yachting marina plus shops, cafés and pubs) in 1973.

BUTLER'S WHARF

Built in 1874, Butler's Wharf was one of London's busiest trading docks for tea, coffee, spice, rubber, spirit and flour. Just over a century later the warehouses were renovated by design guru Terence Conran, and now on the ground floor beneath 98 new luxury flats is a speciality wine and food mall plus a small Conran restaurantopolis: Le Pont de la Tour, Butler's Wharf Chop House and the Blue Print Café. The wharf once handled over 6,000 chests of tea a day, and at the back of the warehouses are the aerial bridges used for bundling bags from building to building.

Docklands

BRAMAH TEA & COFFEE MUSEUM
Open daily, 10-6, adm £3.50,
concs £2, tel 0171 378 0222.

Set up in 1989 by a commodity broker called Edward Bramah, this amazing collection of over 1,000 tea and coffee pots tells the intricate history of the two commodities, from the 17th and 18th-century coffeehouses which spawned the Stock Exchange and Lloyd's Insurance, to that most elegiac of 20th-century inventions, the mass-produced and fast-infusing tea bag.

That most elegiac of 20th-century inventions, the mass-produced tea bag.

THE DESIGN MUSEUM
Shad Thames SE1, open daily 11.30-6
(last entry 5.30), adm £5.25, concs £4,
tel 0171 378 6055.

Created by Terence Conran and Stephen Bayley, the Design Museum is the only museum in the world devoted to industrial design and the cult of consumerism. A bower bird's shrine on the second floor showcases such mass-production classics as the car (including designs by Le Corbusier from 1928), the vacuum (Dyson et al), early televisions and radios, telephones, tableware (by Enzo Mari) and chairs (by Charles and Ray Eames), while the ground floor is devoted to a diverse and diverting range of temporary exhibitions, from Porsche cars to Bosch washing machines.

Docklands

WAPPING

In the 19th century Wapping seethed with seafarers, ship-makers, caulkers, rope and mast-makers, and pirates. The novelist Arthur Morrison vividly evoked its scents and smells: 'something of tar, something of rope and junk, something of ships' stores, and much of a blend of unknown outlandish merchandise. We met sailors, some with parrots and accordions, and many with undecided legs.' Oliver's Wharf, used for storing tea from India and China, was one of hundreds of luxury warehouse conversions in the 1980s. In the same decade Wapping became 'Fortress Wapping' after Rupert Murdoch incurred the wrath of printers and journalists alike when in a single night he disgorged *The Times*, the *Sunday Times*, the *Sun* and the *News of the World* into non-union computerised printing works near Tower Bridge.

THE THAMES TUNNEL & MARC BRUNEL'S ENGINE HOUSE
Open first Sun of every month, 12-4, otherwise by appointment, tel 0181 318 2489.

This 19th-century engine house (near St Mary's Church on the Rotherhithe side of the river) was used to drain the world's first underwater tunnel. Marc Brunel's 1200ft-long Thames Tunnel took 18 years to complete and a catalogue of disasters, human, financial and natural, beset the engineering miracle along the way. The river burst through at least five times, drowning men whose colleagues had already died or been blinded by 'tunnel sickness' (in one of the floods Brunel's son, Isambard, dived in and saved a miner). After it opened in 1843 the tunnel became an instant tourist attraction; stalls selling cakes and ginger beer were set up inside and over a million people paid a penny entrance fee to walk its length beneath the Thames. Brunel's tunnel has since been taken over by the Tube.

Thames Tunnel

Docklands

THE PROSPECT OF WHITBY

Dating from 1520, visited by Pepys, Dickens and Turner, and used as a setting for Arthur Morrison's East End melodrama *The Hole in the Wall*, The Prospect of Whitby is London's oldest riverside pub. A short way downriver from its garden terraces is Execution Dock where pirates, smugglers and felons were chained and hanged in the river until three tides had washed over them. An obstreperous mob turned out to watch the execution of the notorious Captain Kidd: 'I have lain with that bitch three times,' said Kidd, catching sight of one of his mistresses from the scaffold, 'and now she has come to see me hanged.'

LIMEHOUSE MARINA

Limehouse is named after the lime kilns built here in medieval times and fired as recently as 1935. In the 19th century the district was inhabited by shipbuilders, vagabonds and Britain's first Chinese immigrants, and its alien and poverty-stricken streets were frequently evoked in the detective stories of Conan Doyle (Sherlock Holmes) and Sax Rohmer (Fu Manchu). Oscar Wilde's Dorian Gray went to Limehouse to look for opium dens, and Dickens chose it as the setting for the Six Jolly Fellowship Porters ('a tavern of dropsical appearance') in *Our Mutual Friend*. Limehouse has been gentrified in recent years with yachting marinas and luxury redevelopments.

Docklands

It towers over the rest of London and winks at onlookers.

CANARY WHARF & THE ISLE OF DOGS

At 812ft Canary Wharf is the tallest building in the UK (and the second tallest in Europe). It towers over the rest of London and it winks at onlookers. Even for Londoners it seems more like an alien encampment than any recognisable part of London. The tower itself was built in 1991 by the Canadian property developers Olympia & York; it took 18 months to construct and was the first skyscraper in the world to be clad in stainless steel (27,500 tonnes of it). An IRA bomb was set off there in February 1996, killing two people and destroying a million square feet of office space. The tower is now 80% occupied; its two best-known residents are the *Independent* and the *Telegraph*.

In the 19th century Canary Wharf was the main receiver of cargoes from the Canary Islands. Its connection with dogs is more nebulous, though legend has it that the royal kennels were kept on the Isle of Dogs so that monarchs sleeping in Greenwich would not hear their barks.

Greenwich

The ship brought cargoes of tea from India and China, and wool and grain from Australia.

THE CUTTY SARK

Open Apr-Sept, Mon-Sat, 10-6 and Sun 12-6,
Oct-Mar, Mon-Sat 10-5 and Sun 12-5,
adm £3.50, concs £2.50.

The last of the great tea clippers, the Cutty Sark was also the speediest. Launched in 1869, she was specially designed for racing, and in 1871 she won the annual clippers' race from Shanghai to London, completing the voyage in a record 107 days. For the next two decades the ship brought cargoes of tea from India and China, and wool and grain from Australia. The

clipper was named after her own carved figurehead (pictured here) who is dressed in a skimpy 'cutty sark', or short chemise. The name, a corruption of the French 'courte chemise', was taken from the witch called Nellie who sports a cutty sark in Robert Burns' Tam O'Shanter. Moored alongside the Cutty Sark is the Gipsy Moth IV, the 54ft yacht in which the yachtsman Francis Chichester sailed singlehandedly around the world in nine months and one day in 1966.

Greenwich

GREENWICH FOOT TUNNEL

The glass-topped domes on either side of the river are entrances to the Greenwich Foot Tunnel. Built in 1903, the tunnel connects Greenwich to the Isle of Dogs and can be walked through in 4–5 minutes.

THE ROYAL NAVAL COLLEGE
Open daily 2.30-4.45, adm free.

The 18th-century Royal Naval College, with the stately Queen's House looming through the middle, forms one of the handsomest façades along the Thames: the opening scenes of Harrison Ford's *Patriot Games* were filmed here and Greenwich itself, with its photogenic buildings, park and market, is often used for film and TV shoots. The college was originally an austere hospital for disabled sailors, commissioned by Queen Mary in 1696, and was the combined work of three great architects—Wren, Hawksmoor and Vanbrugh. It became increasingly corrupt and in 1873 it closed down and was taken over by the Royal Navy.

Greenwich Foot Tunnel

Greenwich

THE QUEEN'S HOUSE & NATIONAL MARITIME MUSEUM

Open daily, May-Sept 10-5, and Oct-Apr 10.30-3.30, adm, inc entrance to Queen's House, Royal Observatory and National Maritime Museum, £5, £2.50 concs.
NB the Queen's House is closed for refurbishment until November 1999.

The Queen's House, in between the two wings of the Royal Naval College, is an earlier building, dating from 1615 and built for Queen Anne of Denmark. The architect was Inigo Jones, who had just visited Venice and was inspired by his trip to build a palace modelled on the villas of Palladio. His 'house of delights' was simple and classical on the outside, but opulently decorated on the inside with paintings by Titian, Rubens, Raphael, Gentileschi (who did the ceilings) and Van Dyck. The next door National Maritime Museum has a lively display of naval memorabilia ranging from royal barges to the two left-handed gloves and stained uniform in which Nelson died at Trafalgar.

The Royal Observatory was founded by Charles II in 1675 to find a way to measure longitude.

OLD ROYAL OBSERVATORY

Open daily 10-5, £5/£2.50 adm gives entrance to Queen's House & National Maritime Museum.

Here, at 0° longitude east and western hemispheres divide and visitors can straddle the Greenwich Meridian Line with a foot in each time zone. Designed by Christopher Wren, the Royal Observatory was founded by Charles II in 1675 to find a way to measure longitude, the riddle of which was solved elsewhere and almost a century later by a clockmaker from Yorkshire called John Harrison. Harrison built his first marine clock in 1730 and spent a lifetime working on four more prototypes, finally cracking the problem in 1772 at the age of 79 and qualifying at last for the £20,000 reward offered by the Longitude Act of 1754.

Greenwich

THE TRAFALGAR TAVERN

Christopher Wren, Nelson and Dickens regularly dined at the Trafalgar on whitebait, fished from the Thames estuary, and champagne. The tavern reopened after many years in 1965.

TRINITY HOSPITAL ALMSHOUSES

This miniature castle dating from 1613 is the oldest building in Greenwich. The almshouses, with their private chapel and gardens, are run by a City livery company and house about twenty pensioners. One of their more curious possessions is a collection of mummified rats dating from the 1665 Great Plague, when thousands of Londoners took refuge in ships anchored near Greenwich: 'I could not but applaud the contrivance,' Daniel Defoe wrote in his *Journal of the Plague Year*, 'for ten thousand people, and more...sheltered here from the violence of the contagion, and lived very safe and easy.' These days a power station overshadows the almshouses: until the 1930s it supplied electricity for Greenwich's trams and trolley buses.

Greenwich

The global news agency that started out in 1849 as a continental pigeon post.

GREENWICH SILOS

The four silos in this riverside factory are filled with maize and corn. They are used for processing into cooking oil, custard powder, vodka and gin.

REUTERS BUILDING

Designed in 1989 by Richard Rogers of Pompidou Centre fame, this building is the headquarters of the London branch of Reuters, the global news agency which started out in 1849 as a continental pigeon post. The roof, with its small yellow cranes and exposed steel girders, is supposed to look unfinished.

Greenwich

Strong enough to hold a jumbo jet, big enough to hold two Wembley stadiums, tall enough to cover Nelson's Column

THE MILLENNIUM DOME

Entry tickets to the Dome must be pre-purchased, but will be available from September 1999 at more than 20,000 shops and garages selling Lottery tickets, as well as from railway and bus stations

This giant semi-sebaceous cyst will cost £758m, over half of which has been paid for out of the National Lottery. The dome is made of Teflon and fibreglass and supported by 12 steel masts attached to 70 kilometres of wire cable. It is strong enough to hold a jumbo jet, big enough to hold two Wembley Stadiums, tall enough to cover Nelson's Column.

The real test for Dome-hubris, however, comes on Domesday—31 December 1999—when the Dome opens for the first time to the general public and a hostile British media. Entertainments on offer will include a live show, with music by Peter Gabriel, which will be staged six times a day in the central arena. Around this will be the fourteen 'zones', ranging from work, rest and play, to mind, body, spirit and a 'celebration of all things British'

Greenwich

Each of the utopian five-storey houses will be heated by degradable refuse.

sponsored by Marks & Spencer. Visitors will choose between walking through a giant mannequin in the Body Zone, wafting through 'sensory surprises' in the Rest Zone, 'opening their minds' in the Learn Zone, or taking 'a moment to reflect' in the airy-fairy Spirit Zone. Cars are banned from the Dome, and whether anyone will be actually able to get to there via the much delayed Jubilee Tube link remains to be seen. As for the Dome itself, its lifespan is limited to 30–100 years but several film and TV consortia have already put in bids to buy it to use as studios when the millennium celebrations end in 2001.

THE MILLENNIUM VILLAGE

Still a building site and unlikely to be completed until well after the millennium, the Village will eventually be developed into 1,400 state-of-the-art sustainable homes along a 2.2km riverside boulevard. Each of the utopian five-storey houses will be heated by degradable refuse and lit by computerised lighting systems; every resident will have access to the Internet.

Water levels at London Bridge have been rising by roughly 2.5ft per century.

THE THAMES BARRIER

Visitors Centre, accessible by pier, open Mon-Fri 10-5, Sat-Sun 10.30-5.30, adm £3.40, concs £2; includes cafeteria, tel 0181 305 4188.

With its ten gleaming silver hoods, the Barrier is one of the most majestic sights along the Thames. Its gates span 1,700ft of the river, protecting millions of houses from floods caused by powerful tidal surges from Canada (the by-product of low atmospheric pressures

where the warm Gulf Stream and freezing Labrador Current collide) and rising water levels caused by global warming (water levels at London Bridge have been rising by roughly 2.5ft a century).

A committee chaired by John Anderson (of air-raid shelter fame) was set up to deal with the rising water level problem after floods in 1953 drowned 300 people and destroyed thousands of acres of farmland. The idea of a barrier with rotating gates was thought up by

Silvertown & Woolwich

The barrier has been raised 30 times since it opened in 1984.

an engineer called Charles Draper and was inspired by the household gas-tap. In normal conditions the Barrier's gates lie on the river bed on concrete sills weighing up to 10,000 tonnes each. In a flood, yellow hydraulic arms attached to the stainless steel hoods rotate the gates through a 90° arc to form a 50ft-high defensive wall. A staff of 62 mans the Barrier 24 hours a day and the gates can be raised at the push of a button in ten minutes. The Barrier has been raised 30 times since it opened in 1984, and the only collision occurred in October 1997 when a dredger carrying 5,000 tonnes of sand and gravel crashed into the Barrier and sank between piers 4 and 5.

BIRDLIFE

The timber cross-pieces pictured here were put up as perches for ducks and cormorants fishing in the river. Other birds visiting this part of the Thames include great-crested grebes, herons, mute swans, lapwings, terns, redstarts and kingfishers. New reed beds are also being planted on river-walls to tempt back creatures scared away when building works on the Dome began.

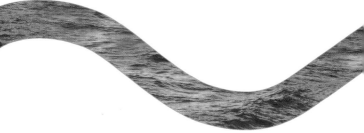

Silvertown & Woolwich

HenryTate founded the Tate Gallery, endowing it with his own collection of pre-Raphaelite paintings.

TATE & LYLE THAMES REFINERY

It was only in the late 19th century that sugar was produced in cubes rather than loaves. Henry Tate snapped up the rights to the German patent in 1875 and opened up this riverside refinery three years later in 1878. The cubes made Tate, a minister's son from Lancashire, a rich man and a generous benefactor. He gave money to scores of libraries and schools around the country and just before his death in 1897 founded the Tate Gallery, endowing it with his own collection of pre-Raphaelite paintings. In 1921 Tate merged with Lyle & Sons, whose golden syrup factory was a mile and a half downriver in Plaistow (both refineries were heavily bombed in the war). Tate & Lyle is now a global concern with interests in fifty countries, from Africa, Asia and Australia to South and North America (where Tate owns Domino Sugar, the leading table-top brand). The planes landing and taking off behind the Thames Refinery come from London City Airport.